A B C Dogs

Kathy Darling
Photographs by Tara Darling

Walker & Company
New York

Dogs from *A* to *Z*

An alphabet book is a good way to learn about dogs. But it is just a beginning. There are twenty-six letters, but there are more than 500 different breeds of dogs.

Why are there so many sizes and shapes? It's because dogs are used for lots of jobs. The dogs that help us herd sheep need long hair to protect them in rain and snow. Sled dogs need strong muscles. Short-legged dogs are the best diggers. Long-legged ones are best for chasing rabbits.

The twenty-six ABC Dogs include those that help farmers and hunters and police. And you will meet dogs with jobs that range from circus clown to guide for the blind. Here are pups to please you and adults that will show you some of the reasons that the dog came to be called Man's Best Friend.

Afghan Hound

"Chase the bunny" is what Afghan Hounds do. Both puppies and big dogs like to go racing and chasing. Afghans are good at running fast and far. If there were Dog Olympics, the Afghan Hound would win the marathon.

Size: large
Color: golden, black, gray, blue, or the striped pattern called brindle
Job: catching rabbits and other small animals

Bulldog

B

Go, Bulldogs, go!
High school and college football teams are often called the Bulldogs. That's because the players want to be like Bulldogs, which are strong and don't quit even if the going gets tough.

b

Size: medium
Color: all-white or white with patches of color, including the striped pattern called brindle
Job: rounding up bulls for a farmer

Cocker Spaniel

Every baseball team should have a Cocker Spaniel. Although these happy hunters are not very good batters, they love to chase pop flies, are great at finding lost balls, and are always willing to retrieve a foul.

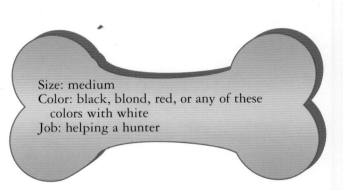

Size: medium
Color: black, blond, red, or any of these colors with white
Job: helping a hunter

Dalmatian

The Dalmatian's nickname is Fire-Dog. You can always recognize these firehouse mascots by their spots. Although every Dalmatian is spotted, each one has a different pattern of colored dots. So even if you had 101 Dalmatians, you could tell them apart.

Size: large
Color: white with brown or black spots
Job: firehouse mascot

English Springer Spaniel

A whistle and a throw toy are school supplies for an English Springer Spaniel. Lessons for these hunting dogs are held in a field, and the spaniel that brings the throw toy back the most times gets the best report card.

Size: medium
Color: brown-and-white or black-and-white
Job: helping a hunter

French Bulldog

F

F is for French Bulldog. It's F-fat. It's F-frisky. And it's F-full of fun. F also stands for friend. That's the job of the little Bulldog with the big ears. French Bulldogs are great at being a kid's best friend.

f

Size: medium
Color: solid colors or the striped pattern called brindle
Job: companion

G German Shepherd

German Shepherds can smell trouble. Police dog Devitt's super sniffer nose saves lives. He is trained to search for bombs. When Devitt smells explosives, he barks so police officers on the bomb squad know danger is near.

Size: large
Color: black-and-tan, all-black, or all-white
Job: helping police, rescue workers, and soldiers

Husky

h

Husky is an Eskimo word that means "big and strong." Teams of these powerful dogs can pull a sled for hundreds of miles across the frozen northlands. When the driver yells "Mush, you Huskies," they show the strength that earned them their name.

Size: large
Color: white with colored markings
Job: pulling sleds

Irish Water Spaniel

Irish Water Spaniels love water. You can find them dog-paddling in the ocean or diving into a lake. They can't even pass a mud puddle without splashing their webbed feet in it. If you have an Irish Water Spaniel, bath time can be a lot more fun!

Size: large
Color: chocolate brown
Job: retrieving things from the water

Jack Russell Terrier

What has four feet, sixteen toes, and will dig from dawn to dark? A Jack Russell Terrier, that's what. There is nothing Jack likes better than digging in the dirt. Unless it is digging in some mud. Nothing is safe underground when this doggy bulldozer sets to work.

J j

Size: small
Color: white with brown or black markings
Job: digging

Kerry Blue Terrier

Kerry Blue — can do.

That's the motto of this terrier from Ireland that can do just about any job that needs doing on a farm. The dusty blue worker, which is born black, can guard the vegetable garden, herd the ducks and geese, and gather the cattle.

Size: medium
Color: bluish gray
Job: helping a farmer

Labrador Retriever

Labrador Retrievers like to help people. They are smart too. Some are smart enough to be trained to guide people who cannot see. If you meet a Labrador Retriever wearing a harness like this one, don't bother him, he's on the job.

Size: large
Color: black, yellow, or chocolate
Job: helping blind people, police, and hunters

M m Mixed Breed

Mixed breed puppies are a surprise package. You can't tell what they will look like when they grow up. There are many mixed breed puppies temporarily living at shelters and humane societies waiting to be adopted. They don't have a fancy pedigree, but their good hearts and sweet nature are more important.

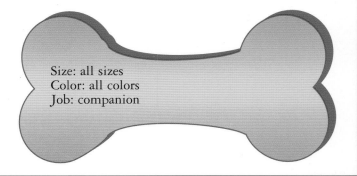

Size: all sizes
Color: all colors
Job: companion

Newfoundland

N

The big black Newfoundland is a lifesaver. If you start to drown, it will swim out and rescue you. Newfoundlands are extremely strong and very brave.

n

Size: giant
Color: black, black-and-white, or brown
Job: lifeguard and protector

Old English Sheepdog

This shaggy dog has no tail. Not even a little one. It is born without a wagger. But you can still tell when an Old English Sheepdog is happy, because it wiggles and waggles its whole rear end.

Size: large
Color: white with gray or gray-blue markings
Job: herding sheep

Poodle

P

Dog shows are beauty contests, and pretty Poodles win a lot of them. Champions like Pom Pom are washed and trimmed into fancy patterns before each show. Sometimes colorful ribbons are tied into their hair.

p

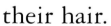

Size: three sizes—small, medium, and large
Color: solid white, black, chocolate, bluish gray, apricot, or silver
Job: circus performer, show dog, and companion

Q Queensland Heeler

"Round 'em up, cowdog." That's what cowboys in Australia say when they need to move stubborn cattle. They know that when the Queensland Heelers start biting the heels of the herd, even the biggest bulls get going.

Size: medium
Color: blue- or red-speckled
Job: herding cattle

Rottweiler

Babysitters-R-Us is the motto of the Rottweilers. They are great watchdogs for children. Not only will they keep guard, they'll also pull a wagon or fetch a ball. A hug and a kiss are their reward. And maybe a dog cookie or two.

Size: giant
Color: black with tan markings
Job: guard, cart puller, and cattle herder

Shar-pei

S

s

Dragon kites and Shar-peis (Shar pays) are both supposed to frighten off evil spirits. The grown-up dog with the built-in frown is scary. But the puppy has so many wrinkles it looks like it was born with the wrong size skin and makes people laugh instead.

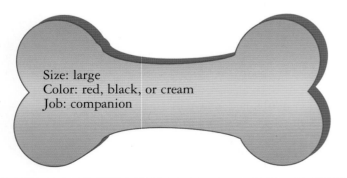

Size: large
Color: red, black, or cream
Job: companion

Tibetan Terrier

Can a dog be a lucky charm? People think so in the Himalayan Mountains of Tibet. They believe that shaggy Tibetan Terriers bring good luck. They feed them special food and give them warm beds. These *are* pretty lucky dogs if you think about it!

Size: medium
Color: all colors
Job: helping to find lost things

U Ukrainian Sheepdog

In the circus, Ukrainian Sheepdogs are stars. Audiences love their silly clown tricks, and the big top rings with applause when they jump through hoops of fire or balance on the back of a galloping horse.

Size: large
Color: white or white with colored markings
Job: circus performer and sheep guardian

Vizsla

The Vizsla
(VEEZ-luh) is a kind of hunting dog called a pointer. When it smells a bird, the dog's whole body stiffens. Its nose points straight to the place where the bird is hiding. A Vizsla can stand for hours without moving.

Size: large
Color: rust
Job: helping a hunter

W West Highland White Terrier

The little white terriers from the west highlands of Scotland are always on mouse patrol. With never-ending energy they check out anything that disappears down a hole—and that includes golf balls as well as mice.

Size: small
Color: white
Job: chasing mice

Xoloitzcuintli

X

It's really hard to say this dog's name (SHOW-LOW-eats-queen-tlee). So most people just call it the Mexican Hairless. Because its naked skin is very tender, the Xoloitzcuintli needs suntan lotion in the summer and a warm coat in the winter.

Size: two sizes—small and medium
Color: black, orange, or light gray
Job: companion

Y Yorkshire Terrier

A Yorkshire Terrier is so tiny that it is called a toy dog. Of course, it is not a toy, but it is small enough to be invited to a teddy bear tea party. Be warned, however! Yorkshire Terriers seldom leave any cake or cookies for the other guests.

y

Size: small
Color: black with tan markings
Job: companion

Zaire Dog

Z

A Zaire Dog can't go "woof woof," "arf arf," or even "yip yap." It's a dog without a bark. African hunters tie a bell around its neck so they can follow it through the rain forest. They call their silent dog Basenji (bah-SEN-jee), which means "wild thing."

Z

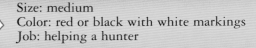

Size: medium
Color: red or black with white markings
Job: helping a hunter

Dog Hall of Fame

Fastest Runner
Greyhound

Best Swimmer
Newfoundland

Tallest
Irish Wolfhound

Shortest
Chihuahua

Heaviest
Saint Bernard

Best High Jumper
German Shepherd

Best Tracker
Bloodhound

Most Popular
Labrador Retriever

Acknowledgments

Thank you to all the people who let us photograph their pets and especially to:

- the working Labradors at the Guide Dog Foundation for the Blind of Smithtown, N.Y.;

- the Dalmatian mascot of the J. H. Ketcham Hose Company of the Dover Plains, N.Y., Fire Department;

- the volunteers and staff of the North Shore Animal Shelter on Long Island, N.Y.;

- and the German Shepherd Devitt, handled by Officer Coyne of the State Police, Troop F, in Monroe, N.Y.

First published in the United States of America in 1997 by Walker Publishing Company, Inc.; first paperback edition published in 2003.

Published simultaneously in Canada by Fitzhenry and Whiteside, Markham, Ontario L3R 4T8

For information about permission to reproduce selections from this book, write to Permissions, Walker & Company, 435 Hudson Street, New York, New York 10014

Library of Congress Cataloging-in-Publication Data
Darling, Kathy.
ABC dogs / Kathy Darling; photographs by Tara Darling.
p. cm.
Summary: Presents photographs and informative text about a different breed of dog for each letter of the alphabet.
ISBN 0-8027-8634-0 (hardcover). — ISBN 0-8027-8635-9 (reinforced)
1.Dogs—Pictorial works—Juvenile literature. 2. Photography of dogs—Juvenile literature. 3. English language —Alphabet—Juvenile literature. [1. Dogs. 2. Alphabet] I. Darling, Tara, ill. 96-40225
II. Title. CIP
SF426.5.D37 1997 AC
636.7'1—dc21

ISBN 0-8027-7665-5 (paperback)

Jacket design for Carl's Afternoon in the Park by Alexandra Day, used on Rottweiler page, upper right photo, copyright © 1991 by Alexandra Day. Reprinted by permission of Farrar, Straus, & Giroux, Inc.

Book design by Marva J. Martin

Visit Walker & Company's Web site at www.walkerbooks.com

Printed in Hong Kong

10 9 8 7 6 5 4 3 2 1